Move to Portugal

How I immigrated to Portugal, and how you can too!

Table of Contents

Introduction

If you're reading this book, congratulations on taking the first step toward moving your life abroad! In addition to traveling all over the world since I turned eighteen, I've spent most of my life living and working as an expat. I had been coming to Portugal for months at a time since 2003. Each time, my trips got a little longer, and it got a little harder to leave. About two years ago, I decided to pack up and immigrate to Portugal. The experience, though not without some hiccups, has been a great one. In this book, I want to share all the things I learned, the things I wish I would have known before I left, and the most wonderful parts of this great country. Keep in mind that my experiences are my own. I am writing this book from the perspective of an American immigrant in Portugal. Some parts of the book, such as obtaining an FBI check for your visa or exchanging your US driver license, may be a little different for you if you're coming from another country. I hope you still find the information valuable. Also, remember that I am not an attorney, accountant, or consultant on Portuguese government affairs. Use this book as a jumping off point on your journey to Portugal. Always consult with a licensed professional before making any important decisions (such as tax or immigration).

Some Facts on Portugal

Portugal is a small country of ten million people in the southwestern corner of Europe. As part of the Iberian Peninsula, it borders Spain to the north and east. The Atlantic Ocean touches the western and southern shores of Portugal. The official language is Portuguese, though English is widely spoken throughout the country. According to the World Bank, Portugal's 2019 gross domestic product was approximately USD $237 billion. Life expectancy in Portugal is over 81 years. This is not at all surprising given the clean air, healthy diet, and tight-knit family structure in Portugal. Approximately 30% of the Portuguese population lives in Lisbon and another 13% lives in Porto. The remaining 57% of the population is spread throughout smaller cities, towns, and rural areas. Portugal has excellent highway infrastructure, though the rail systems could be modernized. Education in Portugal is quite good, with the literacy rate over 96%. Some of the major industries include manufacturing, fishing, and tourism.

Why Portugal?

If you're thinking of retiring overseas or maybe you're just desperate for a change from your life at home, Portugal is an intriguing option for a new home abroad. While it's always been an attractive option for EU citizens, new visa programs and tax benefits offered by the Portuguese government have lured foreign residents from other parts of the world as well. Having made Portugal my home for over a year now, I can fully understand why people choose to come live here. Beaches, mountains, delicious local cuisine, some of the best (and most affordable) wine in all the world, excellent healthcare, and the lowest cost of living in Western Europe all make it a phenomenal place to settle.

Why this book?

This book is designed to provide information to help you lay the groundwork for getting into Portugal, such as securing visas and finding accommodation. It includes important details you'll need for your first six months in the country, such as getting your driver license, securing a vehicle, and shopping for home goods. It also includes suggestions on out of the way places that you can settle here in Portugal. Lisbon is a great city! It's also become a popular and very expensive city. One of the great things about living here in Portugal is taking advantage of the relatively low cost of living. Lisbon is far from a cheap option. Fortunately, there are other beautiful and incredibly affordable options here. Portugal really offers a bit of everything, so you have a great chance of finding what it is you're looking for in this beautiful country.

As wonderful as Portugal has been, like anywhere, it is not without its challenges. While this book aims to highlight all the fantastic things you can experience here and ease your transition to life in your new home, it also seeks to paint a realistic picture of some of the difficulties associated with moving abroad- particularly those you will experience here in Portugal. Like any new place, there's always going to be an adjustment period. Having said that, it's best to go in with your eyes wide open and prepared for the challenges that you may encounter.

The time I've spent here has been a dream! If you choose to make Portugal your home, I hope you'll love it just as much. Let's get started on this new journey…

Chapter 1: Getting Legal – Visas

The D-7 Visa

If you plan to retire in Portugal, you will most likely be applying for the D-7 visa. This is a visa that is available for people who are able to support themselves in Portugal on personal income sources. The D-7 visa allows you to live and work in Portugal. You're not required to leave the Schengen Zone after 90 days, but permitted to stay here continuously.

There are two parts to the application process.

Apply to the Portuguese consulate for a Residence Visa, which allows travel to Portugal for a period of 120 days. You will enter the country on this visa.

During the first 120, one must successfully complete an interview at SEF (the Portuguese immigration authority), after which the Temporary Residence Permit will be granted.

Applying for the D-7 Visa

Your journey begins with your application to the Portuguese consulate. As an American applying from my home country, I made my application in Washington DC. Listed below are the items your will need to complete your application:

Application Form for Schengen Visa

This form must be signed in the presence of a notary.

Statement of Purpose

Here you need to list three reasons why you are interested in relocating to Portugal. This doesn't have to be especially detailed. Acceptable reasons include: 1) an interest in learning the language 2) exploring the beautiful countryside 3) the safety and low cost of living that Portugal offers.

Proof of Income

Here is where you need to show that you earn enough to support yourself in Portugal. This can be social security or government pensions, private pensions, real estate, investments, or even income from a W-2. It should not be income from freelancing. Freelancers should apply for a separate visa that will be outlined below. The minimum wage in Portugal (700 Euros/month) is quite low relative to many other Western countries. You will need to submit a copy of your most recent tax return with your application.

Proof of Funds

You will need to submit your last three months of bank statements. I was told that $15,000 USD is sufficient. This doesn't have to be in a bank account. You can also submit brokerage account statements in lieu of bank statements.

FBI Background Check

You can get more info on completing your FBI check on the FBI's website. You will need to be fingerprinted at a local police station, and submit $18 to the FBI. Your results will be submitted to you digitally. You can print these and forward them with your application.

A Copy of Tax ID Number (NIF)

You can obtain a NIF by having a financial representative go to the Finance office for you. I used a local accountant named Bruno Alexander Afonso (brunoafonso81@gmail.com) and found him to be fast and efficient. His fee was 110 Euros. You will need a NIF to enter into rental or purchase contracts, get a bank account, and conduct all financial business in Portugal- so this is important!

Proof of Accommodation

This was rather easy for me because I had purchased a home in Portugal prior to applying. I simply needed to submit the purchase contract with my application. If you plan to rent, you need to submit a copy of your lease with your contract. It must be a minimum of six months. This means coming to Portugal and securing a place to live. Another option may be to use a vacation website (such as AirBnB) and show that you have accommodation for the six-month period. This will afford you time to look around and find an area you really like.

Proof of Insurance

With a NIF, you can apply for Portuguese health insurance, which is incredibly affordable. I submitted a copy of travel insurance that was valid for 120 days. I used Squaremouth which was incredibly affordable. World Nomads is another option that offers a bit more coverage. If you get travel insurance, you may be required to submit a statement promising to get Portuguese coverage after you arrive. More on Portuguese health insurance in chapter three.

Declaration of Portuguese Criminal Record Check

You will need to sign a paper authorizing the Portuguese police to perform a background check on you within Portugal and submit this with your application.

A Copy of Your Passport and 3 Passport-Sized Photos

You will keep your passport until your visa is approved.

You will also need to include a self-addressed, stamped express mail envelope and a check for the visa processing fees (varies depending on USD/EUR exchange rate). When I applied, my fees were approximately $105 USD.

From receipt of your application, it takes approximately 60 days to process your visa. I received an email saying my visa had been approved. I posted my passport to Washington DC and the passport (with my new visa) was returned in the self-addressed envelope that I'd sent previously. Once you have the passport with the visa, go ahead and purchase your tickets and head off to Portugal!

The D-2 Visa for Freelancers and Entrepreneurs

If you don't have passive income or income from a remote job to support yourself, you will need to apply for the D-2 visa. The distinction between this and the D-7 is important. If you are an employee of a company (and receive a form W-2), you can apply for the D-7 visa. If you are strictly self-employed or plan to start a business in Portugal, then you will need to apply for the D-2 visa. The D-2 visa application is more complicated than the D-7.

In addition to the materials outlined above for the D-7 visa, applicants for the D-2 visa are required to register as a freelancer in Portugal, and you may have to prove that you have the requisite skills and qualifications in that area that you plan to freelance in. If you are an entrepreneur, you will have to submit a business plan along with a pledge to invest a certain amount in Portugal. You will also need to have a company incorporated in Portugal, as well as a deposit in a Portuguese bank to help fund your investment.

In country

Once you arrive in Portugal, you will have to set up a Portuguese bank account (if you haven't already done so). You will also have to set-up an appointment for your immigration interview with SEF.

For the SEF interview, you will need to show your Portuguese bank statements as well as proof of your Portuguese health insurance. I was also asked to provide a deed indicating that I owned my own home here in Portugal. I have heard stories of people enduring quite a grilling during their SEF interview. I used an agent who accompanied me to my interview. More on this below.

Length of Stay

Once granted, your Temporary Residence Permit allows you to stay in the country up to two years from the time that your visa was granted by the consulate. After such time, you may apply to renew your permit for a period of three additional years (bringing your total time in Portugal to five years). After five years, you can apply for permanent residency. After living for a year in Portugal as a permanent resident, you are eligible to apply for citizenship (and the EU passport that comes with it). There is a language requirement for obtaining this.

In hindsight, the visa process is not especially difficult. However, having local assistance can be really valuable. I worked with Timely Solutions in Lisbon (https://www.timelysolutionslisbon.com/).

While immigration attorneys at home can cost thousands, Timely Solutions was incredibly affordable. I paid 650 euros for them to handle everything from the application to enter the country to the required immigration interview during my first few months. Their fee includes the cost of obtaining your NIF. In my opinion, their services are worth it for the interview alone. During my interview, all I did was smile and my representative, Paula, handled the entire process. She answered the questions in Portuguese, submitted the requisite documentation, and I was given my residence permit. NOTE: Her fee was in addition to the processing fee at the Portuguese consulate.

Update: Unfortunately, Timely Solutions, like so many other small businesses, had to close their doors in 2020. There are however multiple other relocation assistance services that work with expats immigrating to Portugal. *Relocate to Portugal* has received positive reviews from many expats and may be able to assist in the migration process.

https://relocatetoportugal.com

Chapter 2: Show Me the Money – Banking & Taxes

Banking

In order to get through your SEF interview, you're going to need a Portuguese bank account. There are tons of banking options here. One of the nice things about Portugal is the use of the MultiBanco system, which allows you to take money out of an ATM without a fee (even if it's not your own bank). Banks also serve as a type of one-stop shop for your financial needs- including issuing auto, health, and life insurance. I was surprised to learn that many banks in Portugal charge a fee for having an account with them. This is usually a small monthly maintenance fee that is charged regardless of the balance that you keep in your account.

Activo Bank is a popular choice because they have no account maintenance fees. They have limited locations, but the branches they do have are open late. As Activo is affiliated with Millennium Bank, you can also do some of your banking at

Millennium branches (which are more easily found in Portugal). Activo is a simple bank that offers fewer services than larger banks. I also have an account with Novo Bank, which offers more services. However, they still charge me a 5 Euro/month account maintenance fee.

Taxes & Non-Habitual Residency (NHR)

UPDATE: Unfortunately, the Portuguese government has passed a new law cancelling NHR. The year 2023 was the last time foreigners were able to apply for this benefit. After December 31, 2023, foreigners will be subject to the same tax laws as Portuguese citizens.

Taxes are always a complicated subject. The information in this section is purely informational and based on my experience. It's always best to speak with a local tax professional in Portugal. I worked with Bruno Afonso (brunoafonso81@gmail.com) and found him to be knowledgeable and efficient. He can assist you with filing your return and ensuring that you are properly registered in the Non-Habitual Residency scheme.

If you are going to be living full-time here in Portugal, you are going to be a tax resident here. Once you arrive in Portugal, you will register with the Finanças office in your town. You will now be in the system as a tax resident in Portugal. The rates in Portugal are quite high. However, you will likely be able to apply for the Non-Habitual Residency scheme (NHR). Until recently, the NHR allowed foreign residents to receive (most) foreign-sourced income tax free. The rate of tax on income that qualifies under the NHR has since risen to 10%, which is far lower than normal tax rates in Portugal. These include your pension income (private or government), W-2 income, income from rental real estate (located outside Portugal), dividends, and interest. While new residents will be responsible for a 10% tax under the NHR, you may be eligible for the foreign tax credit on your American taxes. Check with an accountant who specializes in expatriate taxes to see if this applies to you. By applying the foreign tax credit, your US taxes will be reduced by the amount of the tax that you will have paid in Portugal.

It is important to note that not all income qualifies for preferential treatment under NHR. The capital gains from the sale of shares is taxable here in Portugal- even if those shares are held in an American brokerage account taxable at rates from 28-35%). Any rental income that is earned on property here in Portugal is taxable here in Portugal (taxed at flat rate of 28%). Under the NHR, income from certain professions is eligible to be taxed at a flat rate of 20%. According to the Portuguese Office of

Finanças, the professions on this list are deemed to be scientific, technical, or artistic in nature. This list is updated frequently by the government tax authorities. If you plan to take advantage of this preferential 20% rate, be sure that your profession qualifies.

Applying for NHR

It is so important to note that the time you have to apply for NHR is limited. It is equally important to note that YOU MUST APPLY for this preferential tax treatment. It is not something that is automatically awarded to you based on your residence. YOU MUST APPLY NO LATER THAN MARCH 31 OF THE YEAR FOLLOWING WHICH YOU BECOME A RESIDENT IN PORTUGAL. If you do not apply within this time, you will be subject to normal tax rates in Portugal.

Once you have your residency card (after your immigration interview), you will go to the Finanças office in your town with the residency card and your NIF. You will fill out some personal information and be entered into the system. You will then be mailed a special PIN code. Do not lose this! You will use this to conduct official tax business on the Finanças portal. Even if you have an accountant prepare your returns, that person will need this number. Once you receive your PIN, you can go into the online portal and apply for NHR. The entire application is in Portuguese. If you do not feel comfortable doing this, there are accountants who can assist you. Bruno Afonso (brunoafonso81@gmail.com) provides this service. Depending on the staff in the Finanças office, they may assist you with your application. Bear in mind that they are not obligated to do this. The staff in my town were happy to help me do the application.

Now that you've got NHR, you're set for life, right? Unfortunately, no. The period of preferential tax treatment is only ten years. After NHR expires, you will be subject to the normal taxation rates here in Portugal. Portugal taxes residents under a progressive tax structure.

·   *The lowest marginal tax rate is 14.5% on taxable income up to 7,112 euros.*

·   *Rates of 23% apply on taxable income from 7,112 to 10,732 euros.*

·   *Rates of 28.5% apply on taxable income from 10,732 to 20,322 euros.*

·   *Rates of 35% apply on taxable income from 20,322 to 25,075 euros.*

·   *Rates of 37% apply on taxable income from 25,075 to 36,967 euros.*

· ***Rates of 45% apply on taxable income from 36,967 to 80,882 euros.***

· ***Rates of 48% apply on taxable income above 80,882 euros.***

I cannot stress enough the importance of finding and working with a knowledgeable tax accountant both in Portugal and at home.

Chapter 3: Just What the Doctor Ordered – Healthcare and Health Insurance

When I first moved to Portugal, I received a lot of conflicting information about health insurance- from foreigners living here, from Portuguese citizens, and from employees of the national health system. This chapter simply aims to share my experiences with the process of obtaining private health insurance, registering with the national health system, and accessing medical care. It's important to note that this chapter is only informational and does not guarantee coverage levels or premiums available in the Portuguese market. It's always best to contact an agent or the company directly.

Starting Out

As mentioned in the first chapter, when you apply to come to Portugal on your D-7 visa, you will initially need travel insurance to cover you for the first 60 days. A plan like those available on Squaremouth or World Nomads is sufficient. You may also choose to enroll in private insurance with a Portuguese insurer. After your application is approved, the visa which you are granted is a temporary one that allows you to stay in Portugal until your immigration (SEF) appointment. After your meeting at SEF, your full visa should be approved, and you will receive your residence card in the mail. At this point, you no longer need travel insurance and are able to register with your local health office (*Centro Saude*) where you get your healthcare number (*numero utente*).

Registering with National Health Insurance

Portugal has universal healthcare. Each municipality has its own local health office or hospital. You should register in the town where you are domiciled. If you want to drive in Portugal, you need to register with the national health service as you cannot get a Portuguese driver license without a healthcare number. I was told that the reason is that if you are ever injured in a car accident, the ambulance will only take you to a public hospital. I live in a small town, so the whole process was incredibly simple. I went in, gave them the paper I received from immigration and walked out ten minutes later with my *numero utente*. It's important to note that you **DO NOT** receive a card. The paper you get from your local health office is the only proof of your registration in the system, so **DO NOT LOSE IT**.

Benefits of National Health Insurance

I've been told that as an immigrant here in Portugal, I am entitled to full benefits under the national healthcare system- just the same as if I were born and raised a Portuguese citizen. I've also been told that I am entitled access to the national health service, but at a higher price than Portuguese citizens pay. Finally, I've been told by employees at the health office that even if I were to become a permanent resident in Portugal that I would never have access to the national health service. So… lots of conflicting information. In my experience, I once saw a doctor to get prescription eye drops. I made an appointment (there's a bit of a wait), paid the local price (4.50 euros), got my prescription, and paid a reduced rate at the pharmacy. On another occasion, I made an appointment (again several weeks waiting), paid the full price (35 euros), and paid the full price at the pharmacy. On the second occasion, I was told that since I don't have a social security number in Portugal (which is different from a health number) that I must pay full price. I never argue as I have a good deal here and am happy to pay the little bit extra. Having said that, for major emergencies it is important to have the peace of mind that comes with private insurance.

Even if you don't want top coverage, obtaining private health insurance in Portugal is a sensible thing to do. Regardless of the level coverage offered by the national insurance, the private hospitals are outstanding. What I've been told by Portuguese friends is that the quality of care may vary depending on where you are in Portugal. Apparently, the town I am in is renowned for having some of the worst care in the country. Many Portuguese people living here have encouraged me to go to larger cities to seek care. I've only ever been in the public hospitals and medical offices to refill prescriptions, but their appearance did not inspire confidence. On the contrary, the medical care that I've received at CUF Hospital (several throughout Portugal) has been outstanding. The standard of care is as good as anywhere I've ever lived. With my policy, I've incurred zero out of pocket expenses. Young healthy people may be able to get a limited private policy for 25-30 euros a month. At age 76, my mother pays 300 euros per month for top coverage with MGEN. Do your due diligence, and you should find a plan well-suited to whatever your needs may be. Listed below are several options for private insurance here in Portugal.

MGEN (Advance Care)

I have a very complete policy with MGEN. I pay approximately 130 euros per month for my policy, which is incredibly expensive by local standards. My policy has a zero deductible, offers some coverage for dental and vision, and a 100,000-euro annual policy max. One of most attractive features of this policy is that it covers all pre-existing conditions after a 12-month waiting period. For doctors that accept MGEN or Advance Care, I don't have to pay any upfront costs. For those that do not, I make payment, submit my expenses online, and am reimbursed into my account within 72 hours. I've found MGEN to be fast and efficient. For older people looking for private insurance, I found MGEN to be the most flexible. Another important benefit of my policy is global coverage. However, there are some caveats. I usually need to have treatment preapproved in order for it to be covered.

Allianz

Allianz is one of the most popular choices among foreigners relocating to Portugal. They are affordable, widely accepted, and from what I am told by agents are very cooperative when it comes to paying out claims. The reason I chose not to go with Allianz related to their coverage for pre-existing conditions. I suffer from advanced glaucoma and need to ensure that my insurance will provide coverage for any services I may need related to that. The agent I spoke with indicated that Allianz DOES cover pre-existing conditions provided you can prove that you've had continuous coverage since the onset of that condition. For someone retiring to Portugal who has had the same employer-provided coverage for decades, this may be simple. For someone who has moved around a lot, this may be more complicated. Overall, Allianz is an excellent choice and among the most popular with foreign residents. A very attractive feature of the Allianz policy that I was offered is that they cover medical expenses sustained in car accidents. Many policies do not. You need to consider this when getting your auto insurance policy, which usually includes some coverage for medical expenses.

Fidelidade

I have motorcycle insurance through Fidelidade and in my brief encounters with them, they've been knowledgeable and helpful. They weren't much cheaper than MGEN but did offer some cost savings. Like Allianz, they had an exclusion for pre-existing conditions. The agent that I spoke with said that you can make an application, the company will review your health history, perhaps schedule a medical exam, and then indicate what conditions would be covered or excluded under the terms of the policy. Check with an agent for more information on this. Fidelidade, like Allianz, offered very generous coverage for cancer treatments on some policies (up to one million euros).

Banks

As previously mentioned, your local bank can offer a type of one-stop shopping for your financial needs. I have car insurance through my local bank. They also offer health coverage, too. It may be worth looking into what's available. Millennium Bank has a reputation for offering competitive plans.

Chapter 4: Some Light Housework – Renting or Buying a Home in Portugal

When moving to Portugal, you will need to decide if you want to rent or buy the home you will be living in. Hopefully, you've made at least one trip to the country to begin scouting out areas where you may like to live. Some people fall in love with a place and decide to buy on the spot. They may or may not regret their decision. I would strongly suggest renting for a year before committing to buy. Compared to America, rent in Portugal is relatively affordable. Lisbon is quite expensive, but smaller towns and cities offer a lot of value. I have seen two-bedroom apartments in my city (Peniche) that rent for approximately 450-600 euros per month. This creates a low-cost opportunity to experience the town you want to live in as well as explore other areas without throwing too much money away on rent. It also gives you more time to really explore the real estate market. Look at prices, types of homes, trends in the market and speak to other foreign residents.

What do I need to rent?

Most rental contracts are written for a minimal term of one year. Of course, this does not include vacation rentals. Remember that you will need to present a contract at your immigration interview showing that you have accommodation for at least six months. When you go to rent your home, you will be required to submit your passport as well as your most recent tax return. Many Portuguese residents may require a guarantor. This is a person who guarantees that you will pay the rent. In lieu of a guarantor, they may accept one year's payment upfront. Many people choose to go with a short-term vacation rental prior to renting or purchasing a home. In my opinion, the long-term rentals are much more affordable. What you pay for a six-month vacation rental may be more than what a one-year lease will cost you on a long-term rental. Bear in mind that the agreement must be in writing. A landlord who is reluctant to agree to a written agreement may be trying to avoid taxes. A written agreement protects you and the landlord. It is also required for your immigration interview.

When you secure a long-term rental contract, you will need to hook up all your utilities. EDP is the local electric company, GALP will be for your gas, and you will go to your municipality for water. I've found that monthly utility bills are quite low. Keep in mind that most homes in Portugal do not have heating. Many people use space heaters or simply wear an extra sweater, as winters are fairly mild in most parts of the country. Those homes that do have heat likely have exorbitant heating costs. Energy in Portugal is not cheap. You will need to select a company to hook up your internet, TV, and telephone service. Most companies offer bundles of these services that represent significant savings. MEO, Vodafone, and NOS are some of the larger companies. Once you choose a provider, it's important to go into one of their offices and check what type of internet service is available in your area. If you're working remotely, you will need access to fiber optic internet service (*fibra*). While the internet in Portugal is generally quite good and widely available, it's important to note that some rural areas are yet to offer this. My home is currently served by an ADSL internet connection.

Purchasing a Home

I had been coming to Portugal for several years before moving here, so I had an idea where I wanted to live. The home search, mortgage process, and closing were all pretty simple. Nonetheless, there are a few things that are important to know that should help make your search a bit smoother.

Finding a Home

Before you sit down with a realtor, I recommend beginning your home search on the *Idealista* website. They have homes all over Portugal. This will help you to get an idea of what you get for your money and what's available in the area you're interested in. Having a clear understanding of what's available in the area is very important, as many agents may be hesitant to show you listings from other companies. I viewed listings with a realtor who only showed me her listings. We even passed by other homes with **FOR SALE** signs from other companies. When I asked about viewing those places, she simply said, "It's not for sale." So, it's a good idea to be clear that you want to see all listings in the area. Most agents will agree, as they have systems to split commissions. I've been told by Portuguese realtors that they do have a system similar to the MLS in America. I've also been told that no such system exists in Portugal. Whether there is or not, you don't want to limit your options. Insist on seeing everything that's available and go in armed with as much information as possible.

Signing the Offer Letter

Once I found the place that I wanted to purchase, I needed to sign an offer letter and put down my deposit. Something that my attorney told me (and I do recommend working with an attorney) was that the person selling the home is not obligated to sell the home to the person they contract with. They are free to sell to another buyer. However, they do need to double the amount of the deposit back to the first buyer. I chose to put down a substantial deposit as I really liked the house.

Getting a Mortgage

Upon acceptance of the offer, you need to decide if you are going to get a mortgage or pay cash. I chose to get a mortgage and worked with Novo Bank. There are many banks offering home loans and I found them all to be similar in terms of pricing. The origination fees for my loan were quite cheap (approximately 350 euros). I had a variable rate of 1.64% with a 0.5% prepayment penalty. My bank required a 25% deposit. The home is then subject to a bank appraisal. If it does not appraise at the purchase price, then you will have to put more money down. You may wish to speak to your attorney about inserting a clause in the contract that allows you to get out of the purchase if it does not appraise (or renegotiate the purchase price). Some banks require you to purchase life insurance when taking out a mortgage. I was not required to do so at my bank. It's a good idea to ask about this as you shop around for your mortgage, and factor that into your total cost of credit.

Having gone through the mortgage process several times in the States, I found the process to be far easier here in Portugal. I simply submitted my most recent tax return and documentation proving my employment when I initially applied for the loan. The income threshold was very low. I was required to have 15, 000 euros in annual income for my loan amount. Prior to the loan closing, I needed to submit an electronic transcript of my tax return from the IRS in America. Since I worked with an attorney, I was able to purchase my home while in Portugal and then go back to the USA to get the visa application process started. My attorney handled the closing, signed all the documents on my behalf, and even set up all the utilities in my name. When I returned to Portugal, I simply collected my keys from the realtor and walked into my new home.

Cost of Ownership

In addition to the purchase price and the cost of financing. You are required to pay some taxes upon purchase of your home here in Portugal. The amount of the tax depends on whether it's your primary residence or a vacation home, in a rural or urban area, and the municipality the home is located in. Go over these figures with your realtor, as they can vary significantly. If you are using the home as your primary residence, then your taxes should be lower. Bear in mind that these are not annual property taxes, but one-time expenses associated with the purchase of the home. My home had a purchase price of 130,000 euros and I paid approximately 3,400 euros in taxes on the purchase of the home.

In addition to the taxes involved in the purchase of the home, there are annual taxes to be paid to the municipality where you live. I've found property taxes in Portugal to be far lower than what I was paying in the States. In my municipality, my taxes are approximately 200 euros per year. The tax is set by the municipality and is usually between 0.3% to 0.8% of the **taxable value** (not the purchase price) of the home. Check to see if you are eligible for a three-year exemption of these taxes. Again, I found it very worthwhile to work with a Portuguese solicitor who has detailed knowledge of these laws.

If you have a mortgage, you will most likely be required to have homeowner's insurance with the bank issuing your loan. My homeowner's policy with the bank, which covers flooding and contents, costs me approximately 160 euros per year. I have an additional policy with my homeowner's association. This only costs me about 60 euros per year, but does not cover contents or flooding. The reason I have the second policy is the ease of working with my homeowner's association. My neighbor below me recently had a leak in his bathroom light. The property manager thought it may be coming from my shower. They sent an engineer to come inspect my bathroom and re-caulked the shower. I didn't have to pay any expenses or fill out any paperwork. It was entirely hassle-free. For me, it is well worth the extra 5 euros per month.

My homeowner's association also has a monthly fee. I live in what is considered a condominium or a villa. It's similar to what we would consider an apartment building in the USA. Our building has 11 apartments, a garage, a garden out front, and an elevator. Each resident pays a monthly fee based on the size of their apartment. I live in one of the largest apartments, so I pay one of the highest fees. My fees are 34.50 euros per month. This covers elevator and garage maintenance, as well as regular cleaning of the common areas. Be sure to ask your realtor about condo fees or association dues. Most fees are modest relative to some HOA fees in America. However, they can go up depending on what amenities are offered and need to be maintained. Some of the HOAs in my neighborhood have pools, which require cleaning and maintenance that add to the costs. Be sure to do your due diligence.

Chapter 5: Dude, Where's My Car? – Buying a Car and Getting a Driver License

Depending on where you choose to live in Portugal, you may or may not need a car. If you are planning to settle in Lisbon, you can walk, take the subway, or enjoy the other excellent forms of public transport that the capital city offers. The same is true for Porto. Of course, living in one the two largest cities in Portugal is going to be considerably more expensive than smaller towns or some more rural locations. As you venture away from the big cities, a car becomes a more pressing need. Portugal is an incredibly beautiful country! Having a car here really opens up a world of possibilities and allows you to explore some off-the-beaten-path locations. This chapter outlines the process of exchanging the license from your home country for a Portuguese license, options for purchasing and insuring a car, cost of fuel, and other issues related to driving in this country.

Exchanging Your License for a Portuguese License

The process of exchanging your license is really quite simple, though there are a few hoops to jump through and you need to get started before you leave the States. You need get an apostilled copy of your driver license to bring with you to Portugal. Check and see what steps are required to obtain the apostille in your state or home country. I went to an office store that also offered a notary service. I had my license copied and the notary public signed saying it was an authentic copy. I then mailed it to the Secretary of State in my home state, who apostilled it and sent it back to me. You need this apostilled copy to exchange your license at the Portuguese driver license office or *Instituto da Mobilidade e dos Transportes* (IMT). Just a note: If you are coming from a country where your driver license is not issued in English, you will need to get a certified translation. There are services that offer this, as well as apostilling the translation.

Another thing that you'll want to do before you leave home is get an international driver license to cover you for when you first arrive in Portugal. This is because you cannot get a driver license in Portugal until you get a Portuguese health number (*numero utente*). You cannot get a health number until you get your residency permit (after your meeting with Portuguese immigration- SEF). So, you will be without a license for your first few months in Portugal. If you wisht to drive in the interim, it's best to secure an international driver license. If you don't have a driver license in your home country but plan to get one in Portugal, you will likely need to go to a driving school (*Escola de Condução*).

When you finally have your residency card, you can begin the process of exchanging your license. You need to submit to a health check prior to making the exchange. This will indicate that you are fit to drive. It covers more than your hearing and vision. Though I've been told that how extensive the examination is depends largely on the doctor or clinic you decide to visit. My exam was quite simple. I was given hearing and vision tests, asked a series of questions (pre-existing conditions, medications, etc.), and the doctor took my vitals. The doctor then completes the form online and submits it electronically to IMT.

With your medical clearance submitted, you go to the closest IMT office. Unlike health offices, not every town has an IMT, so you may have to travel a bit. When you get to the office, the attendant will take the apostilled copy of your license, make you fill out some paperwork, take a photo, **and take**

possession of the license from your home country. **You cannot get this back**. You are given a temporary license (a sheet of paper) that will serve as your license until your card arrives in the mail. The temporary license that I was given was valid for 60 days. I was told that it would take approximately 120 days for my real license to arrive. So, that means going back to the IMT before the first 60 days is up and requesting an extension for a further 60 days.

It's important to be mindful of your travel plans when exchanging your license. If you plan to travel back home and need to rent a car, you can do so on a Portuguese license. However, many car rental companies may not accept a temporary license. I was faced with this situation, and the IMT staff were kind enough to present a workaround. I was able to get my temporary Portuguese license and keep my American license for my trip back home at Thanksgiving. However, you absolutely need to turn in your American license at the IMT when you get back from your travels. I forgot to do this, and it delayed the processing of my Portuguese license.

Don't put off the exchange of your driver license. You have only 185 days from the time of your SEF interview to exchange your license. After that, you will need to go through the process the same as any Portuguese person would.

Finding a Car

Cars in Portugal are not cheap! There are a lot of taxes on the purchase of a car here. Of course, you will first be tasked with deciding between a new or used car. Just like back in America, if you buy a new car, you are going to get hit with steep and immediate depreciation. If you buy a used car, you risk buying someone else's problem. There are a variety of used car dealerships that have fairly new cars coming from car rental agencies. These may be an option. *Stand Virtual* and *Car Century* are two that come to mind. Stand Virtual is a type of one-stop shop that connects you with dealerships all over Portugal. Many of these cars come with a limited warranty. Another option is to view the pre-owned stock at local dealers. This can often result in a savings of thousands of euros. As with any used car purchase, it's important to do your due diligence. I opted to purchase a new car when I arrived.

The process for purchasing a new car was fairly simple, though not as easy as back home. At home, you can walk into a dealership, get credit on the spot, phone your insurance company, and walk out thirty minutes later with a new car. My experience here was more drawn out. I went to the dealership and chose the car that I wanted. It did not have a license plate (as most new cars don't), so I had to wait about five business days for the dealer to receive the plates. Once I chose the car, I made my initial deposit (usually 500 or 1,000 euros). Then, I took the information for the new car to my bank to receive auto insurance. I got a VIP policy which included a zero deductible and a total new car replacement provision. I paid about 600 euros for the year. Cheaper policies (with less coverage) are available. When the plates arrived, the dealer called me. I simply wired the remaining balance of the purchase price to him, and I went to pick up my new car.

Financing

If you are interested in purchasing a new (or used) car and require financing, you should check with your local bank. They may offer more attractive rates than dealers. I was quoted a price from a dealer which seemed quite good. As we sat down to discuss the particulars, it became clear that the car needed to be financed at a rate of 7.5% to receive the discounted purchase price. Rates on auto loans are not as affordable as rates on homes. Keep that in mind as you shop around for the car you want and the financing you may need.

Fuel

Fuel costs in Europe are high, and Portugal is especially high. I recently traveled to Spain. At the time of my trip, one liter of *gasolina* was 1.19 euros. This is equal to about 4.45 euros per gallon or USD $5.28 per gallon at the current exchange rate. Portugal is even more expensive! The price of one gallon of gas in Portugal at the current exchange rate is USD $6.70 (or 1.51 euros per liter). You will definitely want to take this into consideration when deciding what type of vehicle to purchase. Many cars here run on diesel. Diesel is cheaper than gasoline and these engines burn less fuel. While the EU pushed diesel engines as an environmentally friendly solution to air pollution in the late 1990s, there are concerns about diesel's impact on the environment. For me, I chose to get a small, gasoline-powered engine.

Tolls

In addition to the cost of fuel, traveling on major highways also makes driving in Portugal expensive. As mentioned in the introduction, Portugal has an excellent highway infrastructure. However, using the highways here has a steep price tag. I live about an hour north of Lisbon. For me to travel to the city center, it is about 5 euros each way. This, coupled with the cost of fuel, puts the price of a trip to Lisbon at about 30 euros roundtrip. A trip to *Cascais* (about an hour and fifteen minutes away) will cost me over 15 euros in tolls plus gas. While it doesn't make the tolls any cheaper, getting a *Via Verde* pass is a great idea. This allows you to go through the tolls without stopping to get a ticket. *Via Verde* passes can also be used to pay for parking, gas, and even snacks in some places. You can get the pass online, by visiting one of their offices (*Autoestradas do Atlantico*) or by going to the *Via Verde* store. The pass has a cost of 0.50 to 0.70 euro per month depending on the option you choose. It's linked to your bank account, so the tolls and other charges are automatically debited from your account each month with a statement emailed to you.

Getting Around

Portugal is a really small country. As I sit in my home on the Atlantic Ocean, I could jump in my car and be in Spain (to the east) in two hours. Having said that, it's probably a good idea to consider getting a navigation system. Of course, *Google Maps* works well. However, bear in mind that your mobile provider will likely have data limits. Also, Portugal has some pretty narrow streets that are better suited to walking than driving. In Leiria, *Google Maps* once took me down a steep path for which there was no way out (just stairs). I had to put the car in reverse and thread a needle to make it out of there without scratching up my new car. Getting a navigation system installed is not a bad idea. Many systems also alert you to speed cameras.

There are not a lot of speed cameras in Portugal, and you likely won't find police setting up speed traps. While it's nice not to have to worry about tickets, cars do travel incredibly fast here. As a native New Yorker, I was originally shocked at how dangerous the roads seemed. Just a friendly reminder to always stay safe and never pass on the right.

Chapter 6: Retail Therapy – Shopping & Shipping

Whether you're buying or renting, you'll want to get your house in Portugal set up the way you like it. There are probably going to be things that you'll want to bring from home to your new home in Portugal. This chapter will cover some things you'll want to know about shipping goods from home, shopping for what you need in-country, and ordering goods from online retailers.

Shipping from Home

Before you begin packing up and taping up boxes, it's important to know that Portugal has some very strict customs enforcement. There are also very high tariffs on the importation of goods from outside the European Union. You have a few options for getting articles from home into Portugal. The first is to apply for duty free importation of household effects. You make this application with the Portuguese embassy in your home country. There are some restrictions as to what can be imported, such as having been in your possession for a year and not for commercial use. The cost of the certificate to import the goods duty free is approximately USD $60. With your application and fee, you must include a detailed packing list. This should include the contents of each box. You must be specific (brand, model number, and even serial number).

A second option is to use an import service from the UK. Though depending on the outcome of Brexit, this may not be an option much longer. Services, such as *First Luggage*, will ship your household effects from the States to Portugal via the UK. The packages will clear customs in the UK and then be sent to Portugal. It should arrive just as any other package from within the EU. You are still required to complete a detailed packing list indicating what you are shipping and in which box. Of course, the UK/EU are now in a transition period that expires at the end of 2020. The future of import laws and taxes remains uncertain. While I know some foreign residents in Portugal have shipped their goods in this manner, I think you still run the risk of either not receiving your goods or being forced to pay a hefty import tax. Remember, whatever option you choose, shipping overseas is not cheap.

The third option is the simplest, and therefore the way I chose to bring what I needed into Portugal. Take advantage of the maximum allowable luggage allowance when traveling to Portugal, and do so for each member of the party you are traveling with. Another good idea is to take advantage of this during your initial fact-finding journey(s). When I came to Portugal to find the house I was going to buy, I brought as much luggage as possible with me. It's incredibly easy and affordable to rent a climate-controlled storage locker in Lisbon (around 20-30 euros a month). I simply stashed my belongings there and went home with empty suitcases. When I came back to stay, I again brought the maximum allowable number of bags.

For your favorite appliances, don't bring them. The power supply is different here. I burned out my coffee grinder and Nutri-Bullet on their first uses. There are going to be some things that you want- some things that you can't bear to leave behind. But remember, if you're starting a new life, you don't want to simply relocate your old life. Bring what you need. The rest you can easily purchase here.

Shopping in Portugal

Portugal really does have everything that you need. There are several large chains of grocery stores, home improvement stores, and electronics stores. Most towns have several mom & pop type stores that offer most of what you need, albeit with a smaller selection. For everything else, there's online shopping.

Groceries

There are several large chains of grocery stores in Portugal. Three of the biggest are *Continente*, *Intermarche*, and *Pingo Doce*. All three have excellent, fresh produce at very affordable prices. They also have a complete deli/butcher section with a great assortment of fresh meats and cheeses. Many offer pre-cooked meal options (such as rotisserie chicken, rice, and potatoes). You'll also find a fresh seafood section, and it's likely whatever you're purchasing was just pulled in by a local fisherman. Portugal offers some of the best seafood I've ever had. As with all places in Portugal, these stores all have great bakeries with fresh bread and pastries.

In addition to these larger grocery stores, there are also some smaller chains that offer a lot of great choices- such as *Lidl*, *Aldi*, *Auchun*, and *E.LeClerc*. I love going to *Aldi*, as they have some brands from *Trader Joe's* back in the States. They also offer a lot of healthy food at reasonable prices. As someone who makes an effort to eat a healthy diet, I've found Portugal to be a really easy place to live and shop. In addition to health food, vegetarian, vegan sections of grocery stores, there is a health food store called *Celeiro* here in Portugal. They have locations throughout the country and offer healthy food options as well as nutritional supplements.

Electronics

Worten is probably the biggest chain store where you can find the electronics you need- including computers, cell phones, TVs, vacuums, kitchen appliances, heaters & air conditioners, and even cameras. They are usually located within *Continente*. Colombo Mall in Lisbon has a huge *Worten*. I've shopped at several different *Worten* locations and found the staff in this store to be incredibly helpful. If they don't have the item you are looking for, they gladly check other stores. If it's available, you can purchase it, and it will be shipped to your store in two to three business days (at no additional charge). I've found some brand names to be expensive here (such as *Samsung* TVs). However, *Worten* offers their own brand, called *Kunft*. *Kunft* items are always considerably cheaper, and I've found them to be of good quality. I purchase most of my home appliances at *Worten*.

Home Improvement

You'll undoubtedly want to pick up a few things for the new home once you arrive. Some big home improvement stores are *Aki*, *Leroy Merlin*, and *Brico Marche*. *Agriloja* is considered a farming store, but they have a lot of home and garden products as well. If you love planting and gardening, then you'll definitely want to find an *Agriloja*. Many of these stores offer renovation or project services. You can pick out the materials in the store and they will connect you with a contractor who does the installation. In many cases, it will be cheaper to find a contractor directly and get them to do the work for you. They can take you to wholesalers for the purchase of materials. Then, you can simply negotiate the installation price with the contractor directly.

Loja Chinesa

You will likely see many stores labeled *Loja Chinesa* (or *Chinese store*). These stores are great! They are independent, family-run enterprises that are similar to a *Dollar General* or *Dollar Tree* type of store back home. They're all-purpose stores that have lots of little things that you may need for the house or just for daily living. Many stores close several hours for lunch in the afternoon, but these stores usually stay open, making them a convenient place to shop when you need something in a pinch.

Sporting Goods

Decathlon is a huge sporting goods store. They are one of my favorite stores here! They have tons of things that you may need for running, surfing, working out, and participating in other sports. They also carry a lot of athletic apparel at great prices. If you need nutritional supplements, you can also find some workout supplements at *Decathlon*. Another popular sporting goods store is *Sports Zone*. These stores are also affiliated with *Continente* and usually located within their stores. Most *Sports Zone* stores that I've been to carry a limited selection of sporting equipment. They mostly have athletic apparel and shoes. As an avid runner, I'm very particular about my shoes, so I need to order them online.

Shopping Online

If you have an *Amazon Prime* addiction, you are not going to be able to satisfy it in Portugal. There is no *Amazon Prime* or *Amazon Portugal* website. Anything that is ordered from *Amazon* in the USA has to be shipped into Portugal and pass through customs. Again, the import duties are quite exorbitant. However, you can shop on other *Amazon* websites throughout Europe, and your goods won't have to pass through customs. I usually shop on *Amazon Spain*, as they offer free shipping on any orders of 30 euros or more. This does not require a *Prime* membership. Some goods are a little more expensive (such as my running shoes), but you can usually find anything you need. *EBay* is another option for online shopping. However, be sure that the goods you are ordering are located within Europe. If you are purchasing from a seller outside the European Union, you are going to be hit with import taxes. Of course, many local Portuguese stores also have online shopping options.

Things You May Want to Take

This list is going to be different for everyone. I'm going to share some of the things that I wish I would have taken a lot of, as they're expensive or tough to get here in Portugal. These are specific to me and my needs. Perhaps they're on your list too!

Running Shoes – I already mentioned this. I pay almost double the price here. If you are a runner and need good shoes, pack a few extra pairs.

Reading Glasses – If you have prescription glasses, don't worry. There are tons of great ophthalmologists and optometrists here. I'm talking about those cheap $1 reading glasses that you can pick up in the USA. Here they run about 15 euros a pair. Throw a few in your carry on.

Lip Balm – Seriously. I use *Carmex* a lot. In *Wal-Mart*, it costs 89 cents. Here in Portugal, it costs 5.50 euros (over USD $6). That's just for one tube! If you use a lot of lip balm, bring extra.

Pain-Relieving Creams – If you use *Tiger Balm* or some type of pain cream, you may want to pack a few tubes. I've found comparable products difficult to find here. You can order online, but it's not cheap!

Cameras and Lenses – If you enjoy photography, you may want to update your equipment before making the trip across the Atlantic. You can easily get everything you want here in Europe, but the prices tend to be a bit higher.

Laptops – Again, you can find anything you want here. However, the prices for the same specs here in Portugal are quite a bit higher. If you plan to work online and need new equipment, update it before you leave.

Deodorant – Grocery stores have pretty big selections of deodorant and antiperspirant. If you are going to live here, you're going to have to get used to the local choices. Since moving here, I've switched to *Nivea* and even *Old Spice*. However, if you have a brand that you are comfortable with, you may want to pack a few extra sticks. On a recent trip back to America, a friend from New York who is living in Lisbon said, "You're going to America? Please bring me *Secret*! As much as you can carry!"

Cell Phones – I purchased an unlocked cell phone from *Consumer Cellular* before I left. They usually offer one of the older models at a discount. For example, I got a *Galaxy S8* for several hundred dollars cheaper than the new model. I was able to use my Portuguese SIM card when I got cell phone service here.

Chapter 7: Are You Gonna Eat That? – Food & Drink

Portuguese food is simple, fresh, and delicious. A Portuguese who traveled to America once asked me why Americans cover their food in sauces. "Here in Portugal, we just use olive oil and a little sea salt." While the dishes are simple, they are incredibly good.

Seafood

Seafood is very popular. Lisbon has a sardine festival every summer, and you can enjoy these delicious treats prepared in a variety of different ways. Traditionally, Portuguese sardines are served grilled. Another very popular choice here in Portugal is *bacalhau* (or what we call cod). *Bacalhau* is a very thick and hearty fish. I once saw it being served in a restaurant and asked the chef what it was stuffed with (when in fact it wasn't stuffed at all). You can enjoy *bacalhau* in a variety of ways. While I'm not a big fan of this fish, I think it's best when it's fried. Other popular seafood choices include *dourada* (sea bream), sea bass, and the *sopa de peixe* (fish soup).

Meats

As someone who doesn't eat red meat or pork, I am probably not the authority here. However, pork, beef, and chicken dishes are quite common in Portugal. Cured meats, such as *prosciutto* are often served as appetizers or snacks.

Bakeries (Pastelerias)

Portuguese *pastelerias* are nothing short of amazing! One of the nicest things about living here is that it always seems there's a great bakery within walking distance of wherever I am. I live in a tiny town, and we have three great *pastelerias*. The fresh bread (*pão*) is fantastic. There is the traditional white bread, several varieties of darker breads (*pão mistura* or simple brown bread, *pão integral* or wholemeal bread, & *pão de centeio* or rye). In addition to these traditional choices, you may also find *pão amarelo* or yellow bread made from corn. You'll see many Portuguese stop in a bakery for breakfast and order fresh bread with butter or a slice of ham and/or cheese.

While I bet they are not the healthiest things in the world, the pastel de nata (or Portguese egg tarts) are amazing! Another favorite of mine is *pão de Deus* (or the bread of God). It's a small roll topped with coconut sprinkles. There's no shortage of muffins or cookies, too!

Coffee

Portuguese are serious about their coffee! A simple espresso shot (*um café*) is what you'll see most people drinking here throughout the day. Portuguese espresso is very strong. In most cafés, um café costs anywhere from 65 to 80 cents. For latte lovers, you can enjoy *meia de leite* (literally 'half milk'), which is half coffee and half milk served in a mug. For those who find a *meia de leite* too strong, you can ask for *um galão*. *Um galão* is a glass of steamed milk with a little bit of espresso. I'm partial to a *pingado* in the morning. It's a shot of espresso touched with a little bit of milk.

Wine, Spirits, & Beer

Portugal is well-known for its wine (*vinho*)- and with good reason. I once joked with a friend that when living in Portugal, it's so easy to pretend that you know wine. You can walk through the store, pick up any bottle of wine and say, "This is a great wine!" Chances are you're going to be right. Not only is wine so incredibly drinkable here, it is very cheap. You can easily go out and find a great bottle of wine for 3 to 5 euros. Grocery stores usually have huge selections of wine. *Continente* always seems to have great sales on wine (40-70% off). I recently bought a bottle of Guarda Rios Gold Edition for about 6.50 euros (normally 18 euros a bottle). *Alentejo*, *Douro*, and *Lisboa* are some of Portugal's most famous wine producing regions.

Portugal is also famous for its port wine (*vinho do Porto*). Port is a fortified wine that is from the northern part of Portugal (where the city of Porto is located). It is served in small glasses often as an after-dinner drink. Another famous liqueur here in *ginja*. This cherry liqueur is often served in edible chocolate cups and is incredibly sweet. The city of Óbidos (very close to where I live) has an annual *ginja* festival in April. If you choose to visit Óbidos (which you should), you'll find countless vendors selling this sweet drink (and the chocolate cups) for a euro or two. While it's a bit sweet for my liking, it is something to try.

Portugal has two main brands of beer-*Sagres* and *Super Bock*. *Sagres* is from the southern part of the country (the city of Sagres is located in the Algarve) and *Super Bock* is from the northern part of the country (near Porto). While both are very drinkable beers, I much prefer Super Bock. Beers in a bar (outside of Lisbon) are affordable. Usually you can order an *imperial* (25-cl or 8-ounce glass of draft beer) for about a euro. Several bars in my town have happy hour specials of 50 to 70 cents for an *imperial*. If you are a craft beer lover (*cerveja artesanal*), you won't find the same selection as you would back in America, but you will find some very drinkable craft beers. Lisbon and Porto both have growing craft beer industries. Taking a weekend trip to either city to enjoy some of the local breweries is a must for craft beer fans. *Super Bock* makes a series of beers called *1927*, that are decent. Their *Bengal IPA* isn't overflowing with hops, but it beats a *Sagres* any day. They also offer a *weiss*, *dunkel*, and *rice lager*. Other microbreweries that have bottled beer for distribution throughout Portugal include *Nortada*, *Musa*, and *Sovina*.

Tipping

Tipping is such a common part of American culture that it is often difficult for us to realize that people in other countries don't tip. In some cultures, it can actually be offensive. Tipping is not uncommon in Portugal. In fact, many cafés have tip boxes at the cash register. However, leaving 20-25% of the bill is quite uncommon here. As my Portuguese friends have explained, if the bill is 19.05 euros, you can leave a twenty-euro note and allow your waiter or waitress to keep the change. A two-euro coin is considered very generous as a tip at most restaurants in Portugal. Portugal is still a developing country, and many people who work in the food service industry do not earn great salaries. They won't be offended if you tip, but don't feel it's expected of you. A friend of mine who is a waitress always notes that she loves when people from North America eat at her restaurant. She was shocked to find some of them leave five or even ten extra euros after they've paid for their dinner.

Time to Eat?

Things move slower here in Portugal. This is a major adjustment depending on the life that you're used to back home. Growing up in New York, we used to leave for ski trips at four o'clock in the morning and stop by the local bagel shop for a coffee and a bagel on our way. You won't find anything open for breakfast at that hour. Most *pastelerias* open around seven in the morning- one in my town opens at six. If you need something very early, you can stop by a 24-hour gas station. They almost all serve coffee, and some serve pastries.

Lunches are long. While it is not consistent with what you'll see in Spain (with shops closing for several hours for *siesta*), many stores will close for two hours in the afternoon for lunch. This is usually between one and three in the afternoon. Most stores that take an extended lunch break will usually remain open until six or seven in the evening.

If you are one of those people who loves going out for your early-bird special at four-thirty in the afternoon, then you will have to adjust to Portuguese dinner hour. People here eat late. Growing up, we always had dinner some time between five and seven in the afternoon. Here in Portugal many restaurants don't open until six or seven in the evening. People usually eat at some point between eight o'clock and ten o'clock at night. One of the good things about this is that if you get to a restaurant when it first opens, you'll easily find a table and get very attentive service. My favorite restaurant opens at six-thirty in the evening. It's always easy to get a great table!

Chapter 8: The Honeymoon Is Over. – Challenges to Living in Portugal

Living in Portugal is great, but it's not simply a life filled with cheap wine and ocean views. Like anywhere else, there are challenges to living here. This chapter isn't meant to turn you off to living in Portugal, but just to raise your awareness to the fact that there are things that aren't always easy.

Language

The Portuguese language is REALLY difficult- particularly the pronunciation. I thought after one year that I would be conversational. Instead, my Portuguese language skills are awful. I spent a few weeks in Spain last winter, and someone remarked that my Spanish was better after three weeks than my Portuguese was after six months. In the area of Spain I visited very few people spoke English. It was great because I was forced to work on my language skills by trying to negotiate meaning. In Portugal, almost everyone speaks English. Not only do most Portuguese speak English, but they speak it very fluently. You really can get by here without ever learning the language. That's nice when you first arrive and need to get things done. However, when you are really trying to learn Portuguese, it's tough. I've tried speaking to people in Portuguese and they often say, "Just speak to me in English, please." I get the feeling that if I am ever going to learn this language, I need to enroll in language school courses.

Professional Opportunity

I live on the Silver Coast of Portugal in a tiny fishing village. It's incredibly beautiful. However, it's also outside of a major metro area. I'm fortunate to work online and have income from abroad. If all or even some of that income dried up, I would be in a tough spot. I'm a teacher and in other places that I've lived, there were always tons of teaching opportunities and ways to make extra cash. Here that is definitely not the case. There are really no teaching opportunities in my town and the larger towns further away would not offer much more. If you need the security of having well-paid job opportunities where you live, consider bigger cities in Portugal- such as Lisbon, Porto, or even Coimbra.

Social Opportunity

Living in a small town there is always going to be less to do than in a big city. Unlike the lack of jobs, which is all year round, the town I live in is actually a socially vibrant place to live in the summer months. July and August are incredibly busy with people from all over the world. However, these people are largely just passing through. After the summer months pass, it becomes increasingly difficult to find opportunities to socialize. I'm lucky that there are a few expats in my neighborhood that I've been able to connect with. However, it's important to consider this when you're choosing a place you want to live.

The *MeetUp* app is fantastic and a great way to meet both locals and expats. However, most of their events are located in Lisbon. Before Covid-19, I was driving down to Lisbon every other weekend to have more opportunity to go out. If you are looking to lay down roots for the long-term, consider the bigger cities mentioned above or some other smaller cities and towns, such as *Torres Vedras* or *Ericeira*. You may even think about going down to the *Algarve*.

Time Moves Slowly

I cannot stress this enough. Things move very slowly here in Portugal. The one thing that I do find over and over again is the different concepts of time that Americans and Portuguese people have. On several occasions, I've gone to the post office to mail a letter and had to wait for forty-five minutes. I have been waiting for fiber optic internet service for nearly a year and a half. For a year and a half, my internet service provider has been telling me, "It's coming in about three months."

Service

Many people who've immigrated to Portugal talk about poor service here. I don't think that's a fair assessment. I have received poor service here, but I've also received excellent service here. However, getting people to come and do work on the house has been a major issue. I have made several appointments with different contractors who simply haven't shown up. When you contact them, they apologize, set a new appointment, and often fail to show up again. At first, this really bothered me. I have since grown to accept it. When I first moved here, I hired a painter to do the inside of my house. He called to tell me he was done and give me the bill. I thought, "Wow! He finished very quickly, and the bill was only half what I thought it was going to be!" When I went to check his work, I saw he only painted half the house. I asked when he was going to finish, and he said, "I'm finished now." I called and messaged him to come back, but wound up having to hire someone else to complete the work.

Chapter 9: Where to Now? – Locations

Lisbon has become such a popular destination for people from all over the world who want to immigrate to Portugal. As a result, the price of real estate in Lisbon has gone through the roof. Home prices and rents are outrageous and (depending on where you are relocating from) may not offer much of a cost savings. Having said that, Lisbon is an amazing city! If you can afford it, there is a ton of social and professional opportunity there. You can also enjoy more of a variety in food, the arts, entertainment, and everything that big cities offer. I've chosen to make my home about an hour north of Lisbon on the Silver Coast of Portugal. I'm going to share some of the differences between Lisbon and the Silver Coast, and then introduce a few out of the way destinations in Portugal that you may want to explore.

The Benefits of Living in Lisbon

Internet

This is incredibly important for those who plan to work remotely while living in Portugal. Fast internet is everywhere in Lisbon. On the other hand, getting fiber optic service can be a real issue in some more rural parts of Portugal. Small towns close to where I live offer fiber, but my small town does not.

Energy

There is so much to see and do in Lisbon. It has the 'feel' of a busy city. As a result, I always feel so motivated and productive. When you're around people who are always working and moving, it puts you in that same state of mind. You also come into contact with people who are entrepreneurial and successful. In small town Portugal, that's something that is exceedingly rare. Portugal is the poorest country in Western Europe. In my town, most people make the minimum wage of 700€ per month. Living in such poverty is not easy. As a result, you can see it in the faces of the people and feel it in how they carry themselves.

Diversity

Portugal has a well-known colonial history. As a result, you see many immigrants from former African colonies like Mozambique and Angola in Lisbon- not to mention the thousands of immigrants like myself who've come to make this country home. Portugal also has a booming tourist industry. Most tourists make Lisbon their jumping off point. As a result, you come into contact with people from all over the world. This is less common in my small town.

Socializing

In Lisbon, I've had the chance to meet up and hang out with people from all over the world. It's not just the expanded access to social opportunities, but it's the type of people that you're going to have contact with. I've had dinner or drinks with people who had interesting and exciting careers, people who were entrepreneurs, and those on exciting journeys of their own in life. By contrast, my sleepy little town has a dearth of such residents. People who get a good education and who have big dreams usually take off for somewhere else- either a large city like Lisbon or Porto, or outside of Portugal. As I mentioned, many of the people in my town have jobs that don't offer them very much. They may be working in a café or a grocery store and that's all they will likely ever do. It's difficult to connect with these people that don't have much on the horizon.

The Benefits of Living on the Silver Coast

Cost of Accommodation

Absolutely no comparison here. Lisbon is EXPENSIVE!!! Small studio and one-bedroom apartments (and I mean SMALL) are expensive in Lisbon. I saw a few places on *Idealista* that were listed for around 150k€ and only about 26 meters squared. By comparison, my condo in *Consolação* has a two-bedroom downstairs (115 meters squared) and a separate studio upstairs (16 meters squared) for only 130k€. The same place in Lisbon would likely go 2-3X that price. My place is actually expensive for this part of Portugal. Many small flats can be found for less than 100k€.

Rents are pricey too in the capital. A friend of mine just rented a nice two-bedroom flat in Areeiro for 1,000€ per month. By comparison, my friend here in Consolação has a one-bedroom flat with an ocean view for 350€. Another friend of mine has a one-bedroom flat in Peniche for only 300€. There are other expenses that add to the cost of living in Lisbon, but accommodation is the most glaring difference.

Parking

Parking in Lisbon is difficult and can be expensive. When I travel to Lisbon, I often stay close to *Rossio* square. Underground parking is available. However, it costs 48€ PER DAY! You are able to rent a spot by the month for just under 200€. You can also rent a spot by the month for overnight parking only and that is just under 100€. Bear in mind that this was in the very center of the city and prices may be more affordable as you move away from the center. Many places have street parking that is free overnight. Parking in *Alfama* is free all day (except Tuesdays and Saturdays). Metered street parking usually has a four-hour max.

Traffic

It goes without saying that there is going to be more traffic in a big city. What makes Lisbon traffic so tough is the tiny, narrow streets, which are also quite hilly. It can be difficult to drive. The fact that most cars here have manual transmissions only magnifies the problem. By comparison, my little town offers tons of free parking and almost no traffic.

Nature/Ocean

Lisbon is a coastal city and so is my little town. If being by the beach is a 'must have' on your list, then the Silver Coast may be the place for you. *Peniche* and *Consolação* are awesome, but other spots like *Areia Branca* and *Nazare* are beautiful beach towns as well. If you want to be closer to Lisbon, but also want to be by the beach, look into places like *Carcavelos, Estoril, Caixas,* and even *Cascais.* I have a short and quiet walk to the beach every morning, and I would never trade that for big city living.

Other Considerations

Food

Wherever you go in Portugal, you're likely to find good food. The food is fantastic and affordable. Lisbon offers a lot more variety of course- including pricier options. If you enjoy going out to eat or having drinks out, you will likely experience the higher costs of dining in Lisbon. I always enjoy eating out in Lisbon. I love having the opportunity to put on some nice clothes and go out to dinner at a few nice restaurants. The atmosphere is fantastic. Having said that, the fish and the glass of wine that I pay 25€ for in Lisbon doesn't taste any better than the fish and wine I pay 10€ for in my small town. If you're after variety, then Lisbon is a clear favorite.

Safety

Portugal is a really safe place. Big cities always have the reputation of being more dangerous and that's probably true of Lisbon when compared to small towns on the Silver Coast. Despite this, I have never felt unsafe while in Lisbon. Portugal has very liberal drug laws, and the thing you probably notice most is people trying to sell you drugs on the street- especially in the city square. These people are more annoying than they are dangerous. If you just say, "No thank you," and keep walking, they don't bother you any further. When I'm in Lisbon, I go running alone around 4:30 AM, and I have never felt unsafe. There are times that I walk around at night carrying my laptop and never give it a second thought. Again, this is a close call, but I'll give it to the small town on the Silver Coast.

Now that I've shared some of the differences between Lisbon and the place that I've chosen to live here in Portugal, I'm going to introduce some small towns throughout Portugal that make beautiful places to settle. I'm going to start with my own town.

Consolação

Location

Consolação is a small beach town located one hour north of Lisbon. It's on the Silver Coast of Portugal, five minutes south of *Peniche* and about fifteen minutes north of *Lourinhã*. The lifestyle here is centered on the beach, with fishing, surfing, and beachgoing being commonplace.
Consolação is totally a summer town. There are year-round residents here (like me), but it's night and day from summer to winter. In wintertime, you'll find many shops closed. The ones that are opened often open later and close earlier. Some taverns and restaurants operate on more limited schedules, and some close all together.

In the summer, it's nearly impossible to find parking in some places. The streets, restaurants, and cafes are all packed. Most of the homes here are vacation homes for people from Lisbon and other parts of Portugal. It's also a popular tourist destination for people from all over Europe.

The Beach

If the beach isn't the major draw for you, then you should probably look outside *Consolação*. There are lots of rugged beaches all within a short walk or drive. *Praia da Consolação* is a short walk from my front door. It's packed from July to September, but quiet the rest of the year. Legend has it that the rocks on the beach in *Praia do Consolação* contain huge amounts of iodine that can slow the aging process. As a result, you see many older tourists from all over Portugal laying on the rocks all year round. *Supertubos* beach is less than five minutes driving to the north, and it's about fifteen minutes by car to *Baleal*. Drive south about ten minutes and you get to the beaches of São Bernardino.

Eating & Drinking

There's a great fish restaurant out on the point at *Praia do Consolação*. They serve huge portions of fresh fish, outstanding wine, and it's all super cheap. The way the restaurant is situated, the surfers who are surfing the point are literally taking off on waves right next to you. It's a great place for dinner, drinks, or both. Expect a wait in the summer. *Club da Praia* is the best spot in *Consolação* to catch a sunset. Cheap drinks (good wine and IPAs) can be had and it's super casual. It's actually a temporary, container-style building that's been turned into a restaurant and bar. The owners are really cool. Don't be surprised if after you pay your bill, they say, "One more beer!" and pour you one on the house. The Tavern (or *Taverna dos Arcos*) is a really cool spot for a bottle of wine. It has more of an old Tuscan feel than a Portuguese beach bar vibe, but it's definitely a can't miss in *Consolação*. The house wine will set you back a whopping 4€ a bottle, but spring for a bottle of *Colossal* from Lisbon (10€)- it's still the best red I've had here in Portugal. If you need a bit of upscale living, you can hit up *MH Atlantico*. It's a huge hotel across from the beach in Consolação. A glass of wine will set you back what a bottle would at the tavern, but the food is decent, and the atmosphere is nice. They've also got fast Wi-Fi.

Even the smallest towns in Portugal have *Pastelarias* (bakeries) and *Consolação* has several. *Bom Pecado* has the best bread in town, while *Pão Quente* serves the best coffee. Both have awesome pastries!

Out & About

Running, cycling, and hiking along the cliffs are all easy options here. Of course, surfing, bodyboarding, and kiting are also incredibly popular. *Berlenga Island* is a short ferry ride from neighboring Peniche. The islands are a natural reserve and offer excellent scuba diving (20€ return trip). Expect a slower pace of life outside the summer months. During summer, it's a vibrant social scene and quite easy to meet people from all over Portugal and all over Europe. The villa I live in has three homes on my floor- myself (from New York), my next-door neighbor from Spain, and my neighbor across the hall from Mozambique. Both my neighbors are only here in the summer. I certainly wouldn't say that my town offers a lot of diversity, but there is definitely more diversity in the summer months. While there are a few pubs, there is more nightlife in *Peniche* (ten minutes by car). Even *Peniche* is really a bar and live-music scene. For those who can't do without wild and late nights at the club, they will need to drive to Lisbon.

Work

You'll likely need to either be retired (with a foreign source of income) or to be working online to manage here in *Consolação*. The opportunities are quite limited. Most people work in tourism or agriculture. There are opportunities in tourism, as accommodation here in the summer months can be quite sought after and expensive. Bear in mind that the tax rates in Portugal are quite high and you will need to navigate the process of starting a Portuguese business (or company if you choose to go that route). If you are working online, you'll need to consider the internet infrastructure in this tiny beach town. They still have not installed fiber optic service (though it's promised to be coming soon). At my house, the download is 12 Mbps and the upload is 1 Mbps. If you simply need to send emails, you're fine. If you need something that can support video conferencing, it's not enough. I teach online and rent an office in Peniche- where I have access to fiber optic internet. Even volunteering offers few opportunities here. The local animal shelter frequently seeks volunteers, but they mostly just seek people to walk the dogs.

Costs

Costs are incredibly low. Houses can be purchased for less than 100,000€. New condos are being constructed and at the time of writing many have an asking price of 180,000€- some include a swimming pool. A friend of mine rents a one-bedroom house with an ocean view for 350€ per month. Expect your utilities to be quite low. Most homes in Portugal don't have heating due to the mild winters. If you do have heat and run it in the winter, it will definitely cost you. Internet, landline phone, and cable should set you back about 30€ a month.

What it doesn't have...

Since it's a small town, there's no big grocery store in *Consolação*. There are a few small markets and a farmers' market. If you need a big store, you need to drive to *Peniche*. The major supermarket chains- *Pingo Doce*, *Intermarche*, *Continente*, and *Lidl* are ten minutes from *Consolação* in the town of *Peniche*.

Nazaré

What was once a small fishing village an hour and a half north of Lisbon has now grown into a major tourist attraction in Portugal. *Nazaré* has gained world-wide notoriety for the world records in big-wave surfing that are set off the coast of *Praia do Norte* (or North Beach). In addition to the huge waves, *Nazaré* has become popular with Portuguese and international tourists.

Location

Nazaré is set on the Silver Coast of Portugal. An hour and a half from Lisbon and two hours from *Porto*, this little seaside village is directly between the two largest cities in Portugal. It still maintains the charm of a small Portuguese village. While *Nazaré* really offers everything that you could want or need, some small cities are within a short drive. *Alcobaça* is fifteen minutes away, and *Caldas da Rainha* is only 30 minutes by car. There are three major neighborhoods in *Nazaré*- the beach, the old village, and *Pederneira*.

The Beach

Praia do Norte is the most famous beach because of the giant waves. However, it's also a great out of the way spot to go when the waves aren't big. The long, sandy beaches here are often less crowded than the ones in town. Swimming here can be hazardous as the currents can be very strong. There is also a great deal of camping available near *Praia do Norte*. In the *praia* (beach) neighborhood, there is an endless stretch of white sand beach that is far less rugged than *Praia do Norte*. The main street that runs along the beach is lined with cafes, restaurants, ice-cream shops and *cervejarias* (pubs).

Eating & Drinking

If you want to enjoy a meal or a drink on the beach, check out *A Deriva*. For burgers or sandwiches, *Shoarma* is a great spot. *Adega Oceano* and *Taberninha* both offer great seafood. If you visit the latter, try the shrimp with garlic! *Chocolateria Bom Bom* is a popular spot with locals offering delicious sandwiches in addition to their desert selection. *Sabores*, on the beachfront, is a great place to stop for an espresso. Another thing you can't help but notice as you walk the beachfront is the number of gelato shops there are. Nowhere else in Portugal have I seen so many ice-cream shops! I've tried several and can say that I was never disappointed. Visit *Gelatomania* for delicious Italian gelato. While there's plenty of local Portuguese restaurants and cafes, there is also a fair bit of international cuisine represented. There are quite a few Italian and Indian restaurants in *Nazaré*, as well as a few Turkish kebab shops. *Prediletta* is recommended for pasta or pizza.

Out & About

Nazaré is a very hilly town. In front of the beach is quite flat, but going down to the beach, there is a steep hill. This makes walking or biking a bit more of a challenge, but not impossible. Just keep in mind that you won't always be riding or walking on flat ground. *Nazaré* is a great spot for beach volleyball and, of course, all things related to the ocean. If you're not into surfing the biggest waves in the world, head into sitio (the old village) to watch the huge waves from the cliffs. One of the things that I discovered about *Nazaré* that was really attractive is that the municipal center offers many different types of classes. For seniors wishing to take these classes, they are all available free of charge and include Portuguese language and art classes. Nazare has no shortage of cervejarias- including *A Maltinha*, *Berlim*, and *Irish Pub*. *Irish Pub* offers a pretty good menu in addition to serving up pints of Guinness.

Opportunity

There are a ton of vacation rentals in *Nazaré*- particularly along the beach. For someone who was willing to make an investment and do the work associated with it, there may be some opportunity there. Outside of entrepreneurial activities related to tourism, there is not much available in *Nazaré*. Most areas of the city are well-served by fiber optic internet connections, making online work the easy and obvious choice for those who are not receiving a pension/retirement income from abroad.

Costs

Nazaré is a very affordable option for those looking to buy in Portugal. I saw some beautiful, renovated two-bedroom apartments with ocean views for 185,000€. Another four-bedroom, three-bathroom, luxury apartment listed for 190,000€. A three-bedroom apartment, with a sea view, garage, and terrace was available for 205,000€. There were homes available that were significantly more affordable. However, I wouldn't consider these luxury apartments by any means. They were nice, clean apartments, perhaps just a bit older, and were right around 100,000€. While most homes in Portugal don't have heating due to the mild winters, *Nazaré* is inching further north. Winters can be a little chilly, so you may want to find a place that has heat. If not, a space heater would be something you'd want to have. As I've mentioned in previous destination posts, heating in Portugal is quite expensive.

What It Doesn't Have...

Nazaré has all the grocery stores (*Lidl, Intermarche, Continente,* and *Pingo Doce*) that you could need. There is a ton of shopping in the small alleys of the town. It lacks a major shopping mall, but there are some small cities that are a short drive away. Overall, there isn't much you will go without in *Nazaré*.

São Martinho do Porto

Location

São Martinho do Porto is located about fifteen minutes south of *Nazaré-* the small fishing village that's become well-known around the world for setting multiple records for the largest waves on the planet. It's on the Silver Coast about one hour and twenty minutes north of Lisbon. It is part of the municipality of *Alcobaça*. The closest city is *Caldas da Rainha*, which is only about ten miles away.

The Beach

The major draw of *São Martinho do Porto* is the horseshoe-shaped bay in the center of town. It's got a long, white sand beach that stretches from one end of town to the other. The municipality has done a great job of creating walk trails and footpaths so that people can walk the length of the bay. Houses set up on the cliff on the far side of the bay offer an amazing view (and don't come cheap). As you venture further north in Portugal, winters become a bit cooler. The beach won't be packed during the winter months but expect a huge crowd in summer.

Eating & Drinking

São Martinho do Porto has so many great restaurants and bars right on the beachfront. *Kinara* is one of the best Indian restaurants in all of Portugal and has fantastic al fresco dining. *Restaurante Granada* offers more traditional food. *Restaurante O Farol* is actually on the beach and offers nice seafood dishes. Boca do Mar offers outdoor, upscale dining. If you want something more casual *Waves Pizzaria* has good beers on tap and makes a great variety of specialty pizzas. The Hawaiian pizza is excellent! For live music, check out *Bela Vista*. They have a nice wine list, too!

Out & About

Great hiking and cycling are all within close proximity to *São Martinho do Porto*. Though you could get your exercise every day just by walking the length of the beautiful bay. While the bay doesn't offer surfing, there is a ton of coastline just outside the bay that makes ocean sports possible. Again, *Nazaré* is just a few minutes up the road. While you can't surf, stand up paddle boarding (SUP) within the calm bay is possible. A lot of people just pass time on the beach playing frisbee, rally ball, or badminton. There's a vibrant expat crowd in *São Martinho do Porto*, so there is definitely a social scene to enjoy. A lot of the bars have great live music nights. However, they are packed with expats. If you are looking for a more local vibe, check out *Alcobaça* or *Caldas*.

Opportunity

The opportunities for employment in *São Martinho do Porto* are like most places in Portugal outside of big cities. That is to say that they are limited. There are opportunities for those who wish to move to Portugal as entrepreneurs and start their own business. Many of the restaurants, cafes, and bars on the beach are expat owned and operated. I've spent many weekends in *São Martinho do Porto* and sometimes feel as though I'm actually in the UK. In that respect, it's got an Algarve type of feel to it. Having said that, if you come with a bit of coin in your pocket and are looking to make an investment in Portugal, *São Martinho do Porto* may offer you what you are looking for. As always, do your due diligence.

Costs

Outside of the major cities, you can still find bargain prices on real estate. It's not as incredibly cheap as you might find in some parts of Portugal. Many small, traditional houses can be found for around 130,000 euros. There are tons of building projects. At the time of writing, you could find two-bedroom apartments with a swimming pool for around 175,000 euros. Nicer places seemed to settle in the mid-200s. While luxury units crept up toward 750,000 euros. My impression of the prices in *São Martinho do Porto* was that (like so many other places) when there is a huge influx of expat money, the prices rise to levels that might seem a bit unreasonable to some. Having said that, the bay there is gorgeous to wake up to.

What It Doesn't Have...

São Martinho do Porto has large grocery stores, like *Intermarche*. It also has a local medical center and plenty of pharmacies. It's easy to find everything you need. If you can't get it in *São Martinho do Porto*, then *Caldas da Rainha* is a short car ride. For me, what *São Martinho do Porto* was lacking was authenticity. There are a lot of beautiful, uniquely Portuguese sights on the way in. But being on the beach there, I just felt like I wasn't in Portugal. It has a very tourist feel to it. The set-up is picturesque. It has an Algarve, almost Greek Isle feel to it, but it just didn't feel like Portugal to me. Even the real estate offices on the beach have all their ads in English.

Areia Branca

Areia Branca means white sands in Portuguese and the beaches of this town offer exactly that. It's an idyllic beach town on Portugal's Silver Coast.

Location

Areia Branca is located about forty-five minutes north of Lisbon and just north of the town of *Lourinhã*. It is situated directly on the

Atlantic Ocean and offers some of the longest stretches of uninterrupted white sand on the entire Silver Coast.

The Beach

Areia Branca is definitely livelier in the summer months, but it draws a crowd all year round. It's close proximity to a bigger town (*Lourinhã*) makes it more accessible to many Portuguese people as well as foreign tourists. Pulling into the town, you'll find a small row of shops, including a realtor, as well as a few cafes and restaurants. Regardless of which direction you turn, there are beautiful beaches and great beachfront restaurants. Surfing, bodyboarding, SUP, and beachfront yoga are all incredibly popular in *Areia Branca*. It actually has some of the best beachfront yoga classes in all of Portugal.

Eating & Drinking

One of the drawbacks of being outside of Lisbon is the lack of variety in available cuisine. While you can find codfish on the menu in most places in Portugal, foreign food can be tougher to come by. As soon as you pull into *Areia Branca*, you pass by *Maharani-* one of the best Indian restaurants in all of Portugal. Its manager, Vijay, cooks up some amazing *curries, biryani*, and the best *naan* in Portugal! The service is outstanding, and the waiters will remember your name even after your first visit. Head down to the right and you'll spot *Pizzaria da Praia*, an excellent brick oven pizza spot with views over the ocean. At the other end of the beach, you'll find several great cafes and restaurants, including 100 *Pratus* and *Aquarius*. The restaurant *Foz* is a nice spot to head out for a sit-down dinner or drinks. Great coffees can be had all up and down the beach. Check out *Barraca* for a great coffee or cup of loose-leaf tea.

Out & About

Like many beach towns all over the world, *Areia Branca* boasts many choices for those who pursue an active lifestyle. Running, cycling, surfing, and hiking are all on offer. In the summer, the town is packed and offers a terrific social scene. *Salty Beach Bar* and *Solmar Lounge Bar* are both beach-front bars with great music, drinks, and dancing. Both are also great places to ask about yoga and surf classes.

Opportunity

There is fast internet available throughout *Areia Branca*, which will make remote work an easy option. For those looking to invest, there is enough of a summer crowd to justify an investment in some type of tourism-based endeavor. Outside of remote work and your own entrepreneurial efforts, this town doesn't offer a lot of professional opportunity.

Costs

Costs are low in *Areia Branca*, especially relative to Lisbon. Small apartments can be purchased for just north of 100,000€. One thing that separates this area from other small beach towns is the availability of more expensive, more luxurious housing. A four-bedroom can be picked up for around 350,000 euros. I've seen new luxury villas being constructed for nearly three-quarters of a million euros. Rents are still quite reasonable. You should be able to find a very liveable apartment for around 600 euros. Like most places in Portugal, the utilities are incredibly cheap.

What It Doesn't Have...

Areia Branca is very touristy- for both expats and Portuguese alike. If anything, I think it's missing a small-town, homestyle feel to it. There are smaller groceries stores within walking distance of the beach (*Spar*) and there are larger grocery stores all a short drive away in *Lourinhã*.

Torres Vedras

Up to this point, I've mostly focused on beach towns. Since this is what I love, I tend to spend more time in these places than anywhere else. However, one town that is inland and deserves mention is *Torres Vedras*. I love almost everything about *Torres Vedras*. It's one of my favorite small cities in Portugal. A smaller and beautiful city, not all that far from Lisbon, *Torres Vedras* offers almost everything- except the price tag attached to big city living.

Location

Torres Vedras is located about forty minutes north of Lisbon and it is inland. If you're a beach lover, you won't have far to go. Just remember, *Torres Vedras* is not on the coast, so do away with the idea of those early morning strolls along the beach. However, *Praia Azul* (Blue Beach) is only about twenty minutes by car. *Santa Cruz* is also a fairly short (15-20 minute) drive.

Eating & Drinking

Herein lies the value in being outside a small town and being in more of a city atmosphere. *Torres Vedras* is not Lisbon or Porto, but it does offer a lot of fantastic restaurants and bars. *Taberna 22* is one of my favorite spots. They do terrific fish and have an extensive wine list. The atmosphere is also fantastic. Another great spot that caters to all tastes is *Organik Burger Art Bar*. They offer a great vegetarian menu, as well as meat and fish. Their desserts are terrific too! One of my favorite little bars to stop for a glass of wine is *DOC* (or *DOC Bifanas*). They have a great wine selection, and a few decent beers too. The beer selection varies, but you should be able to find a drinkable IPA here. They also have a small kitchen that does bar food, such as wraps and fries that are pretty tasty. If you're after a more upscale experience, check out *República Wine Bar & Tapas* on *Av. 5 de Outubro*.

Out & About

There are tons of things to do and see in *Torres Vedras*. *Grande Rota das Línhas de Torres Vedras* is a tremendous walking trail that stretches over 100km and offers a window into the town's and nation's history. The trail goes through the countryside where you can pass fortifications that were built to protect Lisbon from invading French forces. The *Castelo de Torres Vedras* is another must see, including the *Church of Santa Maria do Castelo*. The historic district of town (*Centro Historico*) has tons of restaurants, bars, cafes, and shops. This is a great place to go walk around for the evening and stop for dinner. Even though it's a relatively small city, *Torres Vedras* has a small shopping mall called *Arena*. All the major grocery stores, including *Aldi*, are located in *Torres Vedras*.

Healthcare

One of the big draws of *Torres Vedras* is the outstanding private healthcare that is available there. *CUF* has a large hospital in *Torres Vedras*. It is modern and well-equipped with everything you need, and the standard of care is as good as anything that I've experienced anywhere in the world. Bear in mind that this is a private hospital. I can't speak to the *Centro Saude* (national health center in *Torres Vedras*). If you plan to only be on national health coverage, then you should investigate what the *Centro Saude* offers. In my town, Portuguese people often say the standard of care is not as good as other cities. Remember that private insurance in Portugal is a fraction of what it would cost you in America.

Cost

Torres Vedras offers reasonable rents and home prices for those wishing to buy. You should be able to rent a one or two-bedroom flat for approximately 500-600€ per month. Those who want luxury and proximity to the historic district should add to that budget. If you are looking to purchase a home, you can find plenty of homes in need of renovation and repairs. Those looking for a turn-key opportunity, can get a small place for under 100,000€ very close to the center of Torres Vedras. I came across a beautiful, newly constructed one-bedroom in the heart of the historic area. It was overlooking the castle and listed at 125,000€. A newly renovated duplex with a view of the castle listed for 229,000€.

What It Doesn't Have...

I said that I love almost everything about *Torres Vedras*. For me, the thing that's missing is the beach. It's not all that far from Lisbon. It has great healthcare, restaurants and bars, social opportunity, and even a shopping mall. However, I would miss walking across the street to the beach. If you need the beach, consider *Santa Cruz* as a nearby option.

A Quick Look Before You Go...

So, now that we've done a deep dive into five of the best small towns on the Silver Coast, I am going to briefly mention some other town- both here on the Silver Coast and throughout other parts of Portugal. These are places that you may want to explore as you seek out places to settle.

Coimbra

Coimbra is a stunning city. Located inland, it is approximately two hours north of Lisbon. The city has breathtaking views of old churches, monasteries, museums, and a large university. There's also a beautiful river (*Rio Mondego*) that runs through the city. This is one of the big draws of Coimbra. The river is flanked by a beautiful park- perfect for picnicking, running, or just a morning stroll. Proximity to a large university makes this a great spot for younger people looking for a more vibrant lifestyle.

Óbidos

Óbidos is a beautiful walled city, the focal point of which is the *Óbidos Castle*. It was a wedding present from *King Dinis* to his wife *Queen Isabel*. The area around the castle is a tourist hotspot. However, once you move away from the castle, *Óbidos* has a small-town feel. The *Óbidos Lagoon* is beautiful place to spend a Sunday, and there are also great hiking trails in the area. It is also very close to *Praia D'El Rey*.

Praia D'El Rey

For those who can afford it and want a more upscale living experience, but still want to be out of a big city, then *Praia D'El Rey* may be the spot. While not a gated community, when you enter *Praia D'El Rey,* it has the same feel as a private community. There's no graffiti anywhere, and the streets are immaculately kept. It also offers one of the best golf courses in all of Europe. It is on the coast with tennis courts and the Marriot Hotel overlooking the beach. Prices are higher, but so is the standard of living. Bear in mind, this is not close to grocery stores (or much of anything). It's a beautiful, out-of-the-way golf course community on the beach.

Marvao

Marvao is located about ten kilometers from the western border with Spain. When I visited it reminded me of a smaller version of *Óbidos* with fewer people. The town is set on a hill and has breathtaking views. As you drive east from the coast of Portugal, you pass many small towns that would make great off-the-beaten-path places to settle. Again, these are more remote and offer less in terms of services. They may even require longer trips to the grocery store, but they're beautiful, nonetheless.

Santa Cruz

Santa Cruz is a small beach town, and it's not all that far from Lisbon. Located between *Ericeira* and *Peniche* on the Silver Coast, *Santa Cruz* is a popular spot for a lot of younger residents, as well as retirees. It's got a small city center and a vibrant yoga scene. There are lots of great restaurants, such as *Noah*, right on the beach. There is a lot of camping on the outskirts of *Santa Cruz*. While I know several older residents who have settled in *Santa Cruz* and been quite happy, I always considered this town to be a great spot for younger residents. The close proximity to *Torres Vedras* also offers some social and professional opportunities.

Ericeira

This is an incredibly popular spot for young people who love surfing. *Ericeira* is known as the surfing capital of Portugal. It has a vibrant surfing and yoga scene. It is also popular with many 'van lifers,' or people who come to Portugal to live out of a van. Given its close proximity to Lisbon, it is also a popular vacation home spot for many Portuguese. As a result, homes are not as cheap as in other small beach towns in Portugal. However, if you are young, want to be close to Lisbon, and want more social opportunity, then *Ericeira* is definitely a place to consider.

Sintra

Sintra has a microclimate that makes it look entirely different from other parts of Portugal. Driving through *Sintra,* I sometimes think that it almost looks like a northern California forest. With castles and palaces, *Sintra* is a popular place for tourists. However, once you get outside the center, you can really enjoy nature. There's beautiful hiking trails, beaches, and opportunities for cycling. *Sintra* is a popular choice among many young Portuguese who work in Lisbon. *Sintra* is considerably cheaper and very close to the capital (by car or rail).

Closing

I hope this book helped to address any concerns you had about moving to Portugal. More than anything, I hope it got you excited for the next phase of your life. Portugal is an up and coming location for retirees, entrepreneurs, and immigrants from all over the world. It is hands down the cheapest spot in Western Europe, yet still offers so much. The people, the scenery, the food, the wine, the healthcare, the safety, and the affordability should all help put Portugal on top of your list as a place to settle.

Finally, thank you for purchasing this book! Writing is something that I really enjoy doing, and I wouldn't be able to continue to do it without your support. If you enjoyed this book, please check out my other titles listed below.

Obrigado!

Also by James J. Riley, EdS

Journey to the Coast: Coast FIRE, Geoarbitrage, & Financial Independence

Teaching English Online: Leave Home, Live Rich, Retire Early- A How-To Guide for Digital Nomads

Think Success: Fifteen Rules for Establishing and Maintaining a Successful Mindset

Speak Easy: An English Language Activity Book- Beginner Level

<u>Author Bio</u>

James "Jay" Riley is originally from Long Island, New York. He has been an educator for nearly fifteen years and a world traveler his entire life. He holds MBA, MAcc, MA TESOL, and EdS degrees. He has lived, worked, and traveled all over the world, but currently resides in Consolação, Portugal.